emotional
ROOMS

emotional
ROOMS

the sensual interiors of benjamin noriega-ortiz

ATRIA BOOKS

new york   london   toronto   sydney

ATRIA BOOKS

1230 Avenue of the Americas
New York, NY 10020

Library of Congress Control Number:
2006051462

ISBN-13: 978-0-7432-8504-9
ISBN-10:   0-7432-8504-2

First Atria Books hardcover
edition June 2007

10 9 8 7 6 5 4 3 2 1

ATRIA BOOKS is a trademark of
Simon & Schuster, Inc.

Manufactured in China

Design by Mark Byron
and Christine Hwong
Illustrations by Christine Hwong

For information about special
discounts for bulk purchases,
please contact Simon & Schuster
Special Sales at 1-800-456-6798 or
business@simonandschuster.com.

To steven

$\mathcal{A}$cknowledgments

There is no person more committed to this book than my loyal colleague and friend Mark Byron. Without his help I could not have begun to think of putting a book together. With the great help of Christine Hwong, who worked innumerable hours with Mark making sure that every image was beautiful and appealing, we would not have this book. I am grateful to my entire staff and the many specialized vendors who have provided me with the help to produce magical interiors, and to my clients, who have allowed me the honor of spending their money to create art. My family patiently encouraged me to follow my instincts and helped me grow and become the designer I am today. For that and more, I am extremely indebted. To my teachers, who imparted in me the passion to design, especially Jaime Suarez and Jorge Rigau, thank you. And finally my deepest thanks to Rene and Steven, two wonderful beings who at different times have shared their lives with me and who have given me their love and support. Rene gave me the opportunity to design my first houses and the design freedom to play. Steven, who I constantly admire for his sense of style, has trained me to see interiors as enjoyable solutions, whimsical and fun. Through his discerning eyes I look at design with a fresh approach every day. Mil gracias.

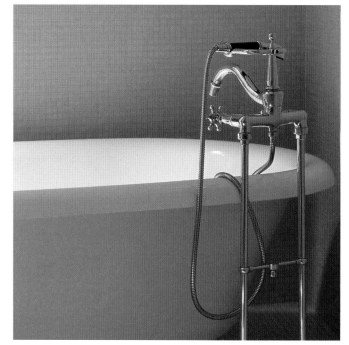

ontents

About

benjamin noriega-ortiz the designer

Born in Puerto Rico, I am the son of an accountant and a nutritionist. For as long as I can remember, I wanted to become an architect. My mother used to buy me graph paper notebooks that I used for drawing house floor plans. My favorite designs were interior courtyard houses. I was eight or nine years old then, and like other kids I played with Legos and Tinker Toys. But in my case the structures I built were life size.

I have a brother with whom I shared a room until I reached puberty. I love my brother, Juano; however, we had nothing in common at the time but the room we shared. Our room had a pair of twin beds with our initials on the surface in big letters (think *Laverne & Shirley*). He spent his leisure time playing sports, a passion he shared with my father. When I was given a room of my own, what a treat that was! I painted the walls pure white. The contrast was beautiful against the shiny black terrazzo floors. I bought one-inch-wide red cloth tape with my allowance that I used to delineate all the corners of the room. My mother made me a khaki-colored bedspread to which she added a red welt, to echo the tape around my room. I placed the bed sideways in the middle of the room against one wall. The space had one lamp on the floor, no table, no desk. I put everything extra in the closet. Eventually, practical matters intruded and I had to compromise and get a table, a chair, a desk, and a table lamp, but I always felt that the original design was better. When I was in my early teens, my parents had two more children, Chelo and Inés María. I became their on-and-off nanny, with sufficient authority to make them finish their Cheerios before getting up from the table. I was also the one who had to mediate when there were conflicts. I love those memories! I grew up with a sense of responsibility, and needless to say spatial awareness, that was nourished all the way to college. We spent every weekend in our one-bedroom apartment on Luquillo Beach, which brought the family closer. I designed the apartment with my mother to suit our needs. It was easy living! Of course, my siblings and I were always outside.

Once I graduated from high school I applied to the School of Architecture at the University of Puerto Rico, but my application was rejected. I never knew why. I tried again. The second time I was invited to take a test, which I passed. I thought I had reached Heaven. Those were magical years when I was introduced to design, art, music, photography, dance, Italian, and so on. I had discovered a world unbeknownst to me in my growing years. I was in my element! I saw Martha Graham perform. Traveled the island to study building types with Jorge Rigau, a young architect who later became the first president of the local AIA chapter and a prominent architecture book author. I made ceramic sculptures with Jaime Suarez, the best ceramicist in the island, who later became a world-known artist in the field. It was exhilarating. As a graduation present from my parents I traveled to Europe for the entire summer of 1980. This was my first time away from home alone and it was amazing. Everything that I had studied in school and read about was right there in front of my eyes. Caravaggio's masterpiece at the Uffizi Palace, Bernini's colonnade in Rome, Venice, the

Pompidou Center in Paris. My eyes were opened to what had only been a fantasy before.

When I returned to PR to continue my studies, I decided that following my master's degree studies I was going to move away from home. I settled in New York City where I completed my second master's degree, this time in urban design, at Columbia University. New York City replaced Europe as my main inspiration. Stanton Eckstut, who designed the magnificently acclaimed master plan for Battery Park City, made me passionate about urban design. I graduated and stayed in NYC working with an architect who needed help. He was from the Aldrich family and inherited clients from his family firm, Delano and Aldrich. However, while supervising a project in Chelsea for Dina Merrill's son, I met a cabinetmaker who at the time was working with John Saladino, who told me that they were looking for a designer. I don't know what prompted me to pay the office a visit the next day with my résumé and give it to him, but I did. Consequently, I was called for an interview and hired immediately. That is when my love affair with interior design started. I found that my diverse background gave me an advantage in getting into this field. I remained with this firm for nine years.

By 1992 I started my own practice and I designed my first piece of architecture, a small house in Amagansett. The house was a small 1,200-square-foot open space with bleached pine floors and seafoam green–upholstered furniture. I designed the house with my former partner Rene Fuentes-Chao in mind. He grew up in Cuba, so he understood the need for a house in which you could go outside from every room. The bed, enclosed in mosquito netting, was perched on a built-in platform that brought the mattress up to the sill of the bay window. The double outdoor shower had a full-length mirror and it was under a fabulous tree. It was magical! The house made the cover of *Elle Décor* that summer, and from then on, more projects received publicity all over the world. Both apartments that I have shared with my partner of eight years, Steven Wine, have been published in such magazines as *New York*, French *AD*, German *Madame,* and others in

America, Europe, and Asia. I have worked on two houses for Norman Lear, in Los Angeles, while being the head designer at John Saladino, and designed two apartments in New York for Laura Esquivel, the author of *Like Water for Chocolate.* And, of course, I worked with rock star Lenny Kravitz—who recently opened his own firm— designing an apartment in New York, a house in Miami Beach, a house on Eleuthera Island in the Bahamas with architect Jackson Burnside, and remodeling his historic New Orleans pad. I have worked for Kohler, for which I designed two model bathrooms; Cartier, for which I designed a store in SoHo; developed a W Hotel on Vieques that was never built; and I am presently developing a hotel for the Morgan Hotel Group. In addition, I've had appearances on HGTV, Fine Living, TLC, and E! And all of this has taught me a thing or two about design. Although interior design must conform to function, the process is more art than craft. You need to balance the human need for comfort with the more satisfying need for fantasy and fun.

emotional
ROOMS

 *Introduction* Interior design books typically fall into two categories. The "how-to" book is the one that "walks" the reader through every step of how to create, say, a feather-covered lamp or a bedroom that feels like the ocean. It would teach them how to install a gauzy curtain to give an office alcove a hint of dreaminess. It would tell them what kind of material to use, where to order it, where to buy the track lighting and how to attach it to the ceiling. The other type of interior design book is for inspiration. This is the idea behind *Emotional Rooms*: inspiration. I'll show you the

sources behind my inspiration to produce my interior design work. I'll encourage and provoke you to look into your own experiences in life to find what will inspire you to produce interiors that you can call your own. I believe that by showing what and how I see, you will come to understand how to use your own experiences. That is the best reference you can use to determine and drive your own design. Often clients become so preoccupied with buying what they think is the perfect sink, just the right sofa, and so on, that they fail to breathe and think about what's best for

the space. The most important and first thing to decide is how you want the room to "feel." When I decide on a strong emotional concept such as serenity, everything else falls into place. Too many instructions can confine creativity, and my designs are about freedom, not confinement. I treat interior design as an art, not a craft. There is no "correct" way to design a room. In fact, the first thing one has to do is to forget the "correct" way.

To accomplish serenity, for instance, consistency of color is extremely important. When you look at furniture as objects with form and color, you remove some of their reality. The objects become individual sculptures that you arrange in space. The shape, color, and feel of an object—rather than preconceptions about its purpose—are what tell an artist where to place it. As the reality goes away, one is able to see things one could not see before, such as the negative space between the objects, which is as important as the objects themselves. One also begins to see that every object has a color, and one starts to treat color as another "object." Once reality—the intellectual idea of what a room is for—goes away, the emotions are free to arrange the room. The result is a space that elicits an emotional response. Therefore becoming what I call emotional rooms.

A room can make you feel calm and serene or agitated and uncomfortable. People are often uncomfortable in their own homes because they choose a variety of furniture and objects that they believe others would accept and be impressed by, rather than what would truly make them happy. They settle for pleasing others and denying themselves the satisfaction of self-indulgence. Life in New York City, where I have been living for more than twenty-five years, is inherently stressful. As a consequence, it's extremely important to come home to a shelter that takes me away from the outside hustle and bustle. When a person gets home, he or she should step into his fantasy, her peace.

process

The four elements of design for interiors are architecture, color, furniture selection, and lighting. Architecture is the space itself. Color brings emotions to the space and is of primary importance. Then you select the objects. The pedigree of furniture is not the key to success—as many would believe. The key is, rather, what the furniture will provide to the space and the inhabitants. Finally, lighting—this is when everything gets revealed. The right choice will either highlight or obscure an object.

architecture

After meeting with a client and establishing the program, it is important to look at the architecture of the space: the structure that defines the void that people fill. Alignment as well as outside vistas are extremely important and should be defined early on. Ask yourself where you will most likely spend your time in the room. And what you see from the room, out the window or door, is almost as important as what you see in the room. The color and feel of the landscape, urban or rural, affects the perception of every interior space. Look at the way the elements in Nature relate to one another. Look at the way the vegetation grows and what direction the sun sets. Imagine that you are in the wild and you have to establish camp. Most likely you will choose the most beautiful view for your sitting area. You will choose to rest where the smells and the sounds are best for you. The freedom that you experience in the wild should be adapted to your needs at home.

color

If you want the room to feel calm and serene, which is my favorite emotion for a room, make sure you repeat one color as much as possible. My favorite color is blue-green. In Spanish I call it *bruma*. This is the color of water at the wave crest when it hits the seashore. It is also the word used to represent haze, mist, or fog. In my experience, abundance of one color produces serenity. Think of how you feel when you are looking at the vast ocean while on a cruise ship. The serenity that you feel is mostly a result of the abundance of one color: blue, green, or blue-green. When the color gets interrupted with too much white, let's say waves, the view is not as serene. This also happens when you look at mountains covered in vegetation. The abundance of green in the lush mountains of Puerto Rico generates a profound calmness.

When choosing a color, remember that color is in everything you see, and that the way you perceive color has a lot to do with lighting. Not only is the lighting that the color provides important but also the way colors reflect one another. John Saladino,

my mentor in interior design and a marvelous colorist, always reminded me of Joseph Albers's famous theory that you can only see color against color. In applying color I use a basic principle, darker rooms should have darker colors, and lighter rooms should have lighter colors. Consider how people look—you included—inhabiting such a room. The result is what will render the environment comfortable for you.

It is important to remember that materials have color and that they help you create a mood. Wood is a color, as well as metal and plastic and so on. If you cover a dark wood chair in blue fabric, the chair is not blue. However, if you paint the wood to match the fabric, the color enhances the expression of the shape, and the object therefore becomes the expression of an emotion. I use translucent fabrics and materials to separate rooms, for window coverings, and even for slipcovers and bedspreads. Translucent fabrics cast a "fog" over the view, which helps in diffusing reality. (Women have known this fact for years and they implement it by the use of hosiery.) These types of fabrics silence colors and form, delivering them to you virtually out of focus. I've heard that in the early days of film, Hollywood studios used to require that a "gauze" or "gel" be placed on the camera lens during close-ups in order to remove imperfections from the actors' faces. That is what I like to do, veil reality's imperfections.

furniture selection

Think of furniture as sculpture and you will open your mind to an infinite world of possibilities. Furniture is no longer a chair or a table, but a combination of shapes and colors. Again, the pedigree of a furniture piece is not what should lead your decision-making. The piece may be rare, expensive, fabulous yet not serve the space. The history of an object, its age or previous famous owner, is not even visible to the eye. This history must be learned and therefore does not exist in the world of emotions. As a result, I dispose of it very early on in the design process. Combining styles is easy. Again, the intellect may object, but if you isolate styles by shape, color, and scale, you will find that they have more in common than you first thought. For example, if you have a collection of furniture from different periods and you upholster them in the same fabric, they definitely will be at ease in the same room. The same if your furniture has curves or angles. The shapes will "talk" to each other. Two very different curved lamps, for example, will find harmony if placed so that the attribute they share in common—their curves—is what is most striking to the eye.

The furniture layout is part of the architecture of the space. Furniture is no more than buildings within an interior urban landscape anyway. When I studied urban design, I learned that the shape of a void is as important as the textures and colors surrounding it, and that what is behind a building is not as important as what you see in front of your eyes. The same principle applies to interior design. When you look at a floor plan, you have to remember that this is not how you experience a layout. You do not experience every room at once, from above. You experience it room by room, from the inside. While your intellect might tell you that all the rooms must agree with one another, what is behind the walls or in other rooms should not concern you—unless you find a way of being in more than one room at a time!

Furniture placement is an art in itself. I like to approach it in two ways: (a) creating conversation groups (the practical way), and (b) creating beautiful sets (the camera-ready way). Depending on the function of the room, you can decide if it's meant to be lived in or seen. Transitional spaces

such as corridors and vestibules can afford to be overtly dramatic. But one needs tranquillity in a bedroom. Often, when I see pictures of beautiful interiors, I know that the room has been created for the camera. It does not mean that everything has been changed. What it means is that, because the camera sees the room in a different way than the human eye, the room has to be composed to reflect what it really looks like in person. By trying my best to see a room the way a camera sees it, I learned to edit and keep only what I consider necessary. When I am designing, I "place" the camera in the room and it tells me if the room is going to be a "wow" room, a cover, or just a footnote room. All the rooms in a house should have a little bit of "wow factor." When you open the door and see a room for the first time, your breath should be taken away. You should not be able to identify particular pieces of furniture or art, the room should be art in itself. And a strong sight should say it all.

lighting

The human eye cannot see without light. Lighting influences the way colors are perceived and therefore is crucial in finishing a room. A successful lighting design uses natural and artificial lighting sources, including fabrics and other materials which themselves provide their own light. When I am determining the way I'll illuminate a space I try to combine at least three kinds of lighting: task, ambient, and whimsical. I have been very successful with the latter—in part with the help of my partner, Steven Wine, and his business partner Michael Landon's company, . . . And Bob's Your

Uncle. They have been creating one-of-a-kind light sources for our projects using a variety of materials—feathers, glass, leather, fabric, sequins, and crystals to mention a few. Therefore, interesting lighting fixtures have become an indispensable part of my interior spaces.

Whenever possible, I like to work with a lighting designer. A good lighting designer will make your interiors come alive by highlighting materials and furniture that otherwise would stay behind the scenes. A combination of lighting types is best:

halogen with incandescent, up-light with down-light, sconces with overhead, and so on. Lighting should not only make the interiors look good but the people, too. There is no sense having a bedroom that inspires calmness and serenity if your face looks terrible in the mirror.

conclusion

My goal is to help you to see and edit your interiors. Real seeing—seeing not with reality but with emotions and imagination—is the key to creating a space that is in harmony with your own emotions. When I was a student of architecture in Puerto Rico, I spent my summers teaching design through ceramics to children at the art gallery Casa Candina. My students' ages ranged from four to about ten. The younger students were always the best because their imaginations had not been hampered by the school system or society. I "learned" to be a child again by just seeing through their eyes. It is my hope that you will come away from perusing this book inspired to design your spaces based on who you are. To do this, many of you will create something that I would never make myself—spaces that agitate, that are frenzied, that induce confusion. However, those will truly be your spaces, a world with a little more fantasy—not that reality is bad, but fantasy is better.

section 1: Diffusing Reality

nightcap.

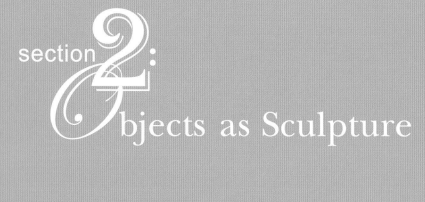

section 2:

Objects as Sculpture

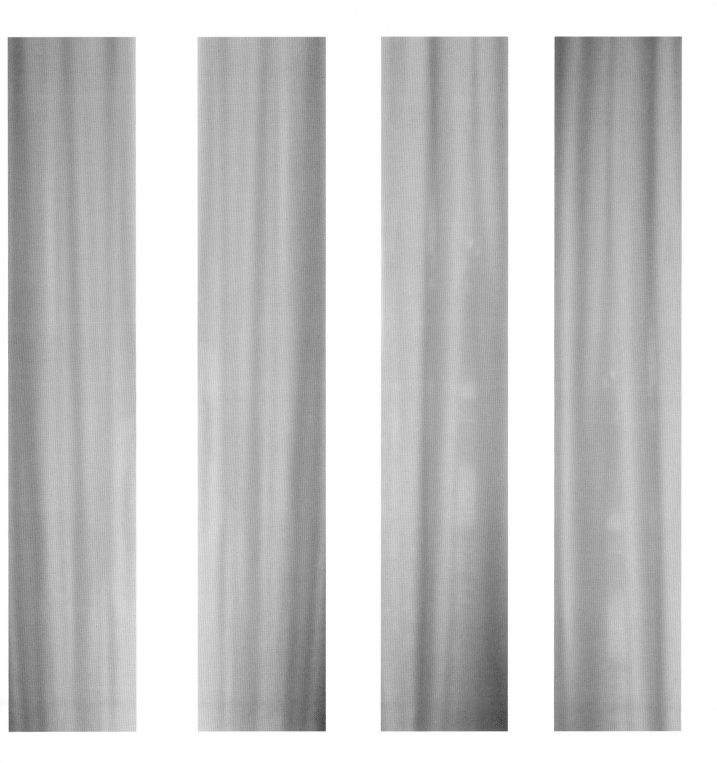

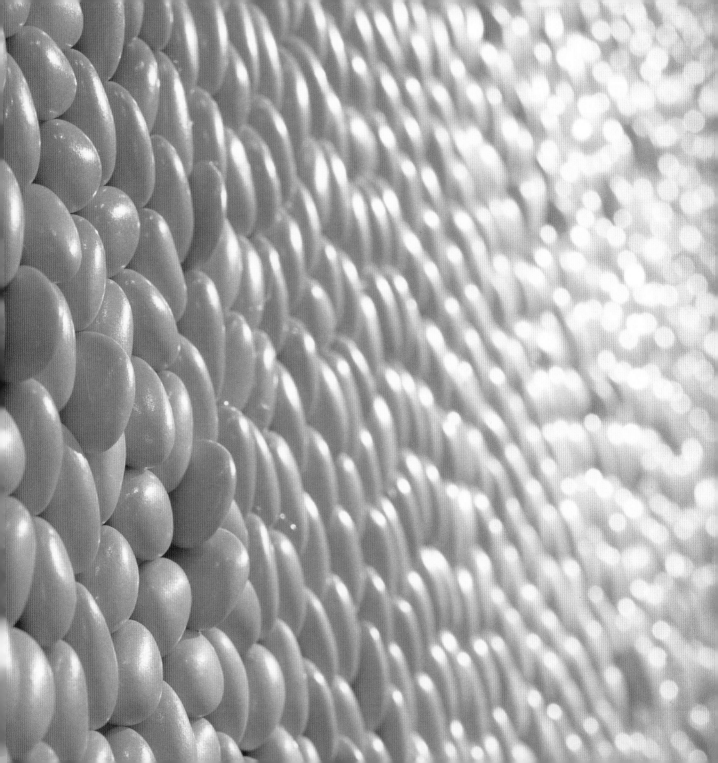

sweet.

110

section 3: Tone on Tone

breathe.

$\mathcal{D}$irectory of photography

photography by quentin bacon, michael luppino, and peter murdock
courtesy of *Metropolitan Home* magazine